THE PHOBIA HANDBOOK

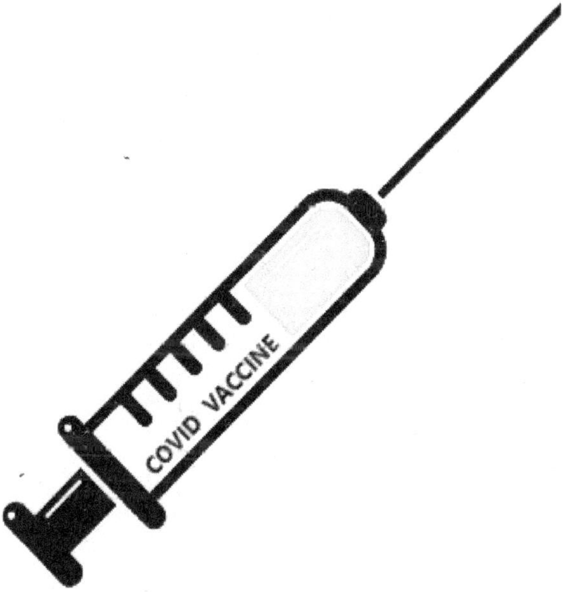

The DEFINITIVE guide to eradicating Trypanophobia – the number 1 cause of preventable deaths on the planet!

KARL ROLLISON

This book is not intended as a substitute for the medical advice of physicians. The reader should regularly consult a physician in matters relating to his/her health and particularly with respect to any symptoms that may require diagnosis or medical attention. If professional advice or other expert assistance is required, the service of a competent professional should be sought.

The advice, strategies and techniques contained herein may not be suitable for your specific situation and are for your information and education only. The publisher is not engaged in professional services, and you should consult with a relevant professional where appropriate. Neither the publisher nor author shall be liable for any loss of profit of other commercial or personal damages, including but not limited to special, incidental, consequential, and or other damages.

Any application of the ideas, techniques and suggestions in this publication are at the reader's sole discretion and risk. The author and publisher expressly disclaim responsibility for any adverse effects arising from the readers actions.

This is a work of nonfiction but, due to client confidentiality, all names have been changed.

For more information regarding Karl Rollison, his products, services, articles and blogs visit:

karlrollison.com

STRESS NINJA ®

Dedicated

To you for reading this book...for being brave enough to admit there is an issue you need to deal with and...

for stepping out of your comfort zone and standing toe-to-toe with your fear.

To Adam Kennard. Emotional well-being therapist

And

Lee Velleman

Thank you for your support and guidance

And, of course

To Suzanne for always being there, and my cat Alien for keeping my neck warm while I write.

CONTENTS

YOU WILL NEED

For this book you will need:

- ***A trusted friend or loved one****
- ***A dedicated day for Chapter 13.***
- ***A syringe with a BLUNT needle*****
- ***A safe, secure environment.***
- ***An open mind.***
- ***To sign the agreement.***
- ***To pay close attention to every word.***

**Obviously someone in your household (during lockdown). If not, a lot of these techniques can be done outside, socially distanced where necessary.*

*** Search the internet for 'Blunt needle and syringe' or 'Printer Ink cartridge refill needle' or 'blunt DIY mixing needles'. They are readily available for a few £/$/€.*

INTRODUCTION

First off, before anything else, I need to give you a virtual cuddle and tell you that you're not weird or strange for having this phobia and later on I'll explain exactly WHY this has happened to you. Secondly, you're certainly not alone; there is various research which indicates that the fear of needles (Trypanophobia) is...

THE NUMBER 1 PHOBIA IN THE WORLD!

One thing I do want you to remember whilst reading this book is that, if you feel anger, confusion, anxiety or frustration then that's good. It means you are taking it seriously. It's not a dull romantic novel with badly developed characters that provokes an indifference to their fate but you have a mild curiosity how it ends...**you need to be passionate about the ending because you are the central character!**

Quick question before we start, from a scale of 0 to 10 (0 being not at all and 10 being extreme) how bad is your phobia?

Write the number here

A Phobia is defined as:

"...an extreme or irrational fear of or aversion to something."

There are basically two main types, complex and simple.

COMPLEX – as the name suggests, aren't straight forward. You couldn't hold a complex phobia in your hand and they, invariably, involve some form of social anxiety like crowds and open spaces. The cause and the trigger can be intricate.

SIMPLE – this is something specific and tangible...something you can point at and identify. These include things like spiders, heights, clowns and, of course, needles.

During my time as a life coach and hypnotherapist I've successfully dealt with phobias all over the world, from the common to the obscure.

If you came to see me at my Harley Street office (not an option at the moment) I could probably resolve your simple phobia in one session. However, I'm not in front of you. You've just got this book so, if you're really serious, you'll need to read it from start to finish and follow ALL the instructions.

Give it your full attention and maintain an open mind.

Some things within these pages may seem strange, repetitive and confusing but don't worry because if you're confused then you're heading in the right direction. Remember:

Your new life is over there...this book will show you how to get there!

Quick quote...

"The main cause of problems for the average person is the ridiculous notion that there is such a thing as an average person."

- K. Rollison

CHAPTER ONE

HOW SERIOUS ARE YOU?

So before we start, how serious are you about getting rid of this fear of needles because I need a bit of commitment from you. If your phobia is so extreme that it prevents you from receiving medical intervention then I would recommend taking it VERY seriously.

If you came to see me I would ask you to sign my mutually binding, water-tight, terms and conditions. It highlights the fact that you have entered into an agreement with me. This ensures that:

A. Everything we discuss is 100% confidential.

B. There must be 100% honesty at all times.

C. I require 100% of your attention.

D. You must follow my instructions to the LETTER no matter how repetitive or confusing.

It's the ONLY way this can work and, be in no doubt that, no matter who my client is or how much they are paying me, if they don't follow my instructions I will simply withdraw my services.

Time is THE most precious commodity we own and the clock is ticking...

During a session I would constantly refer to our agreement to remind the client of their pledge. Obviously, I'm not sitting in front of you, but I still need you to commit to all of the above, so from that perspective I will need you to commit to yourself. Seeing as needle phobias affect everyone around you I want you to commit to this programme in front of those key people. This can be done via a video call if necessary.

Remember: I'm not asking you to restrict yourself from any of life's pleasures, I'm not engaging you in a year-long mission...not even a month, just the time it takes you to follow this book to the letter...a few days.

OR

You could spend a year, 20 sessions and thousands of pounds talking to someone about your relationship with your parents and miss your COVID vaccination window.

So, you've been brave enough to pick up this book, are you brave enough to ***FULLY ENGAGE WITH IT***?

You will need to take responsibility. Read this book and designate a day whilst everything is fresh in your mind. From first opening the book to completing the programme should be no longer than 3 or 4 days at the most. DO NOT DELAY.

Don't be like Edmund Blackadder when he faced a firing squad:

"Can I ask you to leave a pause between the word 'aim' and the word 'fire'?"

"Thirty or forty years, perhaps?"

Don't think it's not relevant signing your name because it is!

It's giving your unconscious mind a clear instruction:-

"I – WANT – TO – BE NEEDLE – PHOBIA – FREE"

The Binding Agreement.

Put this page somewhere prominent in your home. (If you've got the eBook version of this book then print this page)

I ....(your name)

promise to follow EVERY aspect of this short and effective programme to the LETTER and give it my 100% commitment.

I understand that I will be asked to do some strange things but the end goal is freedom from this needle phobia.

Signed... Date ..../......./.........

Witnessed by:

.... Signed....................................

.... Signed....................................

CHAPTER TWO

THE FORCE FIELD

Let me share one of my favourite coaching sessions of all time...

I took to him immediately. He was a big, loud, athletic surfer-type who I estimated to be late thirties early forties. Like all Australians I've met he made me feel really welcome and kept plying me with ice cold bottles of Victoria Bitter. I'd been invited to the party along with the friend I was staying with so I didn't know many people there. Whilst waiting for the alcohol to drag out my 'Karl-the-party-nutter' alter ego I spent the first hour or so people-watching and there were quite a few to watch. The weather in Melbourne that day was beautiful, not too hot with a slight breeze and the air was filled with the wonderful smell of the BBQ, laughter and the splashing of the swimming pool. The Aussies are NEARLY as good as the English when it comes to banter and there was a lot of that in

the air too. After a while I noticed a pattern, most of it was directed at our host. Rob handed me another beer so I took the opportunity to act on my hunch…

"I love your pool Rob"

He seemed to shrink slightly "Err, cheers Karl"

"What temperature is the water?"

"Dunno mate, that's Sarah's department"

Rob took a deep breath in, looked around uncomfortably then said "Look Karl, you'll find out soon anyway coz these idiots won't let me forget it but…I've got a bit of a problem around water"

"I know"

"What? Who told ya?"

"No one, you're a great host and you make sure everyone has a drink and that there are no empty bottles or glasses hanging around. But not once have you been anywhere near the pool."

"Blimey is it that obvious?...Yeah, I've never been in it but Sarah and the kids love it."

"So what happened?"

Rob scrunched his eyes up and ran his fingers through his shoulder-length hair as he relayed the uncomfortable memory:

"Well, I was just a kid. I was a half decent surfer and a strong swimmer but I got caught in a Rip [current]. *I'd been in them before and I knew what to do but I inhaled water, started to panic and nearly drowned. Since then I won't go near the water. I thought the worst thing about it was growing up missing out on messing around in the water with my mates, but nothing is as bad as watching my family having fun in our own pool and not being able to join in."*

"So do you want to keep this phobia? Or do you want to get rid of it?"

Rob turned to face me, took a tiny step forward, slightly leant towards me and became more animated– this is called an 'Ideomotor Response' and was exactly what I was looking for and told me everything I needed to know – he was VERY serious about this subject...

"Oh mate, I can't even begin to tell you how much I want to get rid of it! I've seen doctors, tried antidepressants, been to a counsellor, and I've even had a few goes at therapy but nothings worked...just gotta live with it I suppose."

"Rob, if someone suddenly appeared in front of you right now, cleared his throat, clapped his hands, rubbed them together with a big smile on his face and told you that, if you gave him 60 minutes of your undivided ATTENTION and listened INTENTLY and followed EVERYTHING he said to the LETTER,

that, in one hour you'd happily jump in the water without a care in the world, in front of your shocked family and friends and that you'd NEVER FEAR water again and go on to CREATE thousands of wonderful new memories playing with your family in your FANTASTIC swimming pool...what would you do?"

"Mate, I'd go for it 100%"

I cleared my throat, smiled, clapped my hands and rubbed them together...

An hour later...

Rob had a fixed grin on his face along with the familiar look of confused indifference as he slowly climbed into the swimming pool to stunned silence.

OK so I've exaggerated this story…it actually only took me 45 minutes!

As I mentioned earlier, everything in this book is relevant to your particular journey. I am about to explain exactly why the above coaching session was one of my favourite of all time because that's relevant too!

- Humans love labels. We love to name, measure, compare, quantify and qualify everything. I watched a lot of people recalibrating Rob that day – *"You DO know Rob! Nice bloke…lives in Melbourne…big guy…looks like a surfer, ~~terrified of water!~~"*
- Mocking someone who has an irrational fear might seem like fun but it's not fun for the recipient. Some of the 'fun' was removed from the crowd that day.
- If you have an extreme phobia then it controls your actions. If someone uses that to their advantage then, in a roundabout way, they are controlling you. Rob took control back.

- An extreme phobia is a mental limitation. In some cases they can be as restrictive as a physical one and when we love someone we want them to live without restrictions. There was a lot of love and pride directed at him that day.
- Phobias are heavy, just like shame and guilt. When someone relinquishes them, they grow physically…'a weight off the shoulders'. Great to witness.

From a personal perspective, my favourite aspect of this whole situation was the reaction from Rob's brother-in-law. Apparently, he ran a department of family social workers and he oozed arrogance. He thought the whole thing was staged to showcase Rob conquering his phobia. He'd obviously had too much to drink, was a supporter of certain talking therapies and wanted to find some chinks in my armour:

"Great work Rob but how long have you been planning this? It must have been a while….must have been a good few sessions? 15, 20?"

He then looked at me and said

"I bet you're not cheap either Karl - Pommies usually underestimate how expensive Australia is to live in. I bet you have to charge more than you would in the UK right?"

I was in the pool with Rob and we just looked at each other and started laughing. Rob put his arm over my shoulder and said, ***"Well, actually Luke, Karl doesn't live in Australia and this is the first time we've ever met".***

He didn't believe us but we didn't care...

Like a kid with a new toy (and probably making up for lost time) Rob spent all day in the pool messing around with his family. I joined him in the evening and we continued drinking. He insisted on lamenting his lost swimming and surfing potential but it was outweighed by his joy of being in his own pool. To be honest, I wanted to talk about the classic V8 on his drive but that never happened. He did make one observation that resonated with me and I've shared it with many clients since. Perhaps it'll do the same with you...

"So I'm physically fit and healthy and a great swimmer but the thing holding me back in life was just a collection of thoughts. Thoughts don't actually exist in the real world so my phobia was like one of those invisible force fields you get in Sci-Fi films. There's nothing physically there but it will prevent you moving forward anyway."

Another important thing to remember is that, despite living in a predominately water-sport intensive part of Australia he still managed to lead a happy, healthy life and raise a lovely family. He had ***managed*** his phobia by using avoidance tactics. This is what most people do with their phobias. For example:

- People with spider phobias tend to avoid gardening.
- Those that suffer from a fear of heights rarely go hiking up mountains.

- The individuals with extreme fear of clowns probably don't frequent circuses

I could go on, but you get the picture. Now here's an important thing to remember. Ready?

You haven't got the luxury of avoidance! If you really want a happy, HEALTHY life then you're going to have to overcome it. You have no other options. It's that simple!

"But I've never been ill in my life!" I hear you say?

Well guess what? That won't always be the case and anyway, there's a certain vaccination that you're going to need soon...

The first thing to do is to ***acknowledge*** that you HAVE an issue and then to DO something about it. You're already addressing those points.

But don't focus on the phobia; focus on being without the phobia...

"The secret of change is to focus all of your energy, not on fighting the old, but on building the new."

– Socrates

CHAPTER THREE

PERSPECTIVE

Get Serious...

OK, so I want to go over this again. I'm going to assume you've signed my terms and conditions and if you haven't please do so now. You know, some people in life would rather be proved right than make progress. They would rather stay stuck and act the victim as long as they could say something like:

"See, I followed all the instructions but it didn't work! I told you it wouldn't!"

I know that won't be you because that attitude usually comes from people that don't have the foresight to even realise they have an issue let alone engage in a self-help programme.

I promise that if you stick with this book you will gain back control of your life...

"But I AM in control of my life! I just don't like needles..."

Sorry, but if you have an extreme phobia then you're not FULLY in control of EVERY aspect of your life...***IT is!***

The thing is that anything that causes us extreme anxiety is avoided at an unconscious level. Our brain does this with good intentions in order to keep us safe. Negatives are kept outside of our conscious awareness.

OK, so a needle phobia isn't as controlling as Agoraphobia - at least you can leave the house, but there are still a lot of situations you avoid aren't there!?

If the answer is 'no', then you haven't really delved into it enough but if you're going to get rid of it, you'll need to!

How do I know? Because I've successfully helped people all over the world with exactly the same phobia as you are lugging around. When I start digging, the truth usually comes out and so does the realisation of just how stifling this phobia has been, sometimes evoking tears. Remember, if you have an extreme phobia you'll manage it using avoidance tactics and that includes avoiding:

- Acknowledging that it actually exists.
- Thinking about the consequences.
- Contemplating the alternatives.
- Looking at the direct results.
- Analysing the indirect results.

A few years back a client came to see me at my Harley Street office because he was experiencing massive amounts of stress and anxiety. This was mainly due to the breakdown of his marriage. During the session he nonchalantly mentioned that he had an EXTREME needle phobia but...

"It wasn't a problem...had nothing to do with anything" – His exact words.

I do constant summaries and recaps during a session because the session is never static but constantly evolving and the deeper you dig the more things reveal themselves:

"So, your wife resented the fact that you never take any exotic holidays. So you hate travelling then?"

"No. Not at all! There are Loads of countries I want to explore".

"Your (possibly) soon-to-be ex-wife is constantly moaning [his words] ***about your diet, your lifestyle and your lack of exercise?"***

"Yeah, she signed me up to gyms and is always trying to make me eat healthy rabbit food"

"Have you entertained the possibility that she loves you and knew that, if you did get ill it'd be impossible to get you to see a doctor? Knew that even if you needed a batch of blood tests that wouldn't happen either? Knew that she wanted to share adventures in far off countries but also knew you'd refuse the essential jabs and inoculations needed to enter that country? Maybe her only crime

is caring and loving you but you allowed the fear of a little piece of plastic and metal control your life and potentially destroy your marriage?...in other words maybe IT'S NOT ALL ABOUT YOU!"

OK, not one of my favourite sessions but it all worked out well in the end and they did stay together and they even had a second honeymoon in Thailand... See, successful therapy deals with the *root cause* of the issue not just the *effects* and in this case the seemingly irrelevant needle phobia WAS the root of the problem.

BUT successful therapy involves change and change involves 100% honesty. We can convince ourselves of anything we want but change can only happen when we are honest with ourselves and this involves digging into places that we might want to keep covered. I think stepping up and doing this is THE DEFINITION of bravery. However, like anything else in life, the true magic only happens when we DECIDE to take action so really, because you have this book in your hand...

YOU'RE ALREADY HALF WAY THERE!

So, let's be honest with each other right now. It's probably been holding you back for years now hasn't it? Any of the following ring a bell?

I wish I could have that wart removed.

I stubbed my toe weeks ago and it still hurts. I wonder if it's broken?

That mole seems to be growing.

I'd love to go and see my sister in Canada but it means getting some jabs.

I'm exhausted all the time. I've got zero energy.

These headaches are getting worse.

I've got a good diet so why do I suffer with constant indigestion?

I'd love to see more of the world...

So, whatever the cause of your anxiety, an extreme needle phobia will probably have you lying awake at night worrying more about the inevitable medical procedure than the actual

CAUSE of the problem. The thing is that, anyone living with you will be aware of your anxiety too and if you think this phobia is only affecting you then you're wrong! You're not the only person in your household (speaking metaphorically), your family or your social circle that is affected by your issue. The harsh reality is that...

You need to seriously consider how this affects ALL the people that love and care about you.

Let's flip it: Imagine the person you love most in the world has a toothache. Over the weeks it gets slowly worse. They are popping painkillers like Tic Tacs and they've started drinking regularly too. They're losing weight due to the inability to eat, they're not sleeping and as a consequence they are impossible to live with. The slightest mention of the obvious need for an emergency dental procedure is met with aggression...an impossible situation...

One of the best things we can do as intelligent, caring human beings is to employ empathy and 'choose' to see things from the other person's perspective.

CHAPTER FOUR

WHY ME?

Why do I have this phobia?

<u>Needles – the number 1 phobia in the world!</u>

Forget spiders, heights, clowns, public speaking, crowds, opens spaces or confined spaces...a lot of research around the world lays the title of 'World number 1 phobia' firmly at the feet of the humble needle. I mean, let's face it...

Only drug addicts and those with a needle fetish actually enjoy being stabbed with a sliver of stainless steel. The rest of us put up with it as a necessity, a means to an end.

I've been trying to raise awareness of needle phobias for a long time now. It all started many years ago when I witnessed a close, otherwise very confident, family member having an extreme phobic reaction to an imminent, urgent batch of blood tests. I quickly helped her resolve this and it's no longer an issue but it grabbed my attention and started me on my path. I've now helped hundreds of people around the world and I've also conducted various desk and field research into Trypanophobia. The results are really interesting...

<u>Why it's such a mystery.</u>

The reason people don't realise the extent of Trypanophobia is simply because it's not widely reported. The very essence of the phobia makes it difficult for accurate data collation. Allow me to expand with a very simple but horrifying truth:

Some people (that might include you too) would rather *die* from health issues than receive urgent medical intervention. Also, these same people may well *succumb* to advance terminal illness that could have been detected earlier with a simple batch of blood tests.

Eventually these people could be rushed to hospital for emergency intervention but the doctors will deal with the **issue** not the **cause** (unless it's too late of course). They won't record the fact that the reason the situation got so bad was due to an extreme fear of needles. Also, if the poor patient dies due to complications, and are being examined by a coroner, their deaths won't be recorded as 'death due to Trypanophobia' but instead 'natural causes' or 'undetermined'.

One of the best pieces of research into the effects of needle phobia was carried out by the American supermarket chain 'Target' in 2013. They commissioned the research agency 'Harris Interactive' to conduct an online survey to ascertain why 60,000 Americans annually refuse the Flu jab. They discovered that a staggering 23% of participants admitted avoiding the jab. The reason? Trypanophobia! If that figure is a global representation then...

NEEDLE PHOBIAS ARE THE NUMBER ONE PHOBIA IN THE WORLD!

If you've read any of my other books you'll know that my mantra is:

"Knowledge is power"

In other words, to understand how something works removes the fear of it. So now you know that you're certainly not alone!

If you meet four people then the chances are that one of them could share your phobia, maybe not to your extent, but it could still be a cause of massive anxiety for them. This fact alone should make you feel better. Also, it arms you with a powerful retort if anyone ever questions your phobia:

"Well, actually it's the number one phobia on the planet and a lot of research suggests that it's the biggest cause of premature deaths in the World! So you can shut up!" (That last bit is optional).

Why you have this phobia – Learned behaviour.

No one is born with a Trypanophobia. In fact humans are only actually pre-programmed with two fears: falling and loud noises. The rest are actually learned as we go along. Kids are learning machines and childhood is where we acquire most of our fears and anxieties for the future. I had a phobia of flushing toilets until I was a teenager. Like most disasters in life it was a series of freak events that formed mine. I'd watched a stupid film about a man who drowns after getting trapped in a bathroom that fills with water. This coincided with my dad decorating. He'd loosened the handles of the doors in between coats of gloss and by shear chance (unbeknown to me) the toilet was blocked. So I innocently flushed the toilet and water started flowing over the edge of the pan, in my panic to escape, the door handle came off in my hand. I can still remember it really clearly and it's still one of the scariest moments of my life (and I've been in some VERY volatile situations). My dad (a tough master butcher from East London) heard my screams. He opened the door to find his hysterical young son with tears running down his cheeks and scratches and dents on his newly painted doors. I can still remember the look of pride on his face...

I lived with my phobia until I decided to get rid of it and I did it by using (ironically enough) a process called 'Flooding'. This is a psychotherapeutic method of placing yourself in an extreme situation with the phobia front and centre. In my situation I stayed in a hotel that had a full wet room with a toilet and bidet. I spent a few hours flooding the toilet until I had no reaction at all. I would NEVER recommend this method. When I help people with stress, anxiety, PTSD, phobias, trauma or extreme negative memories (whether I use hypnosis or not) I am constantly monitoring them. I observe every aspect of their being. I will take someone to an extreme but in a controlled manner. You're probably thinking, well what could go wrong? Well, a lot. I was inexperienced when I tackled my fear and did the whole thing standing up, by myself. I could have experienced 'Vasovagal Syncope'. This is fainting triggered by an extreme event which causes a massive change in blood pressure. The bathroom is definitely NOT the environment you want to do that in, it's not considered the most dangerous room in the house for nothing!

So, an innocent little boy, in the wrong place at the wrong time, chose my particular phobia for me. Children, ALL children, are learning machines and a great way of learning what NOT to do is via pain and discomfort. But as a matter of course what do all kids HAVE to endure?

• They need a whole host of vaccinations including Rubella, Measles, Mumps, Meningitis, Tetanus and Diphtheria.

- Milk teeth and wisdom teeth can cause complications so the dentist is required.
- Kids love sweets, so this invariably leads to cavities that requires another trip to the dentist.
- Kids usually have to endure some form of health issue.
- Youth is definitely a great time for broken bones and stitches.

So, all of these things are painful, uncomfortable and stressful and they usually all start with the same thing – an injection. Just like Ivan Pavlov's dog knew it was dinner time when he rang a bell, the children associate the tiny shaft of stainless steel (which in itself isn't painful) with extreme pain and discomfort.

<u>Why you have this phobia – Evolution.</u>

OK, so even though we aren't born with a needle phobia we can still be instinctively wary of them because of what they represent – they are an object that is used to compromise the integrity of our skin, our outer protection against the external environment. Think about it, for millions of years, even

BEFORE we were humans, any scratch or open cut could be potentially life threatening. The only thing we had in our defence was the efficiency of our own immune systems. It was only when Alexander Fleming discovered Penicillin in the early part of the 20th Century that an infection didn't necessarily mean a death sentence.

ANYWAY, what I'm trying to say is something that has provoked tears in the past from my frustrated and anxious clients and it's reminiscent of the powerful scenes between two fantastic actors in one of the best films of all time... In 'Good Will Hunting' Robin Williams tells Matt Damon:

"IT'S NOT YOUR FAULT!"

Quick Quote...

"Regrets are like trying to sail with the anchor down or drive with the brakes on...they will stop you moving forwards."

–Karl Rollison

CHAPTER FIVE

KNOWLEDGE IS POWER

Half-time recap.

You should now be feeling better about your phobia:

- ***It's a lot more common than you thought – you're not alone.***
- ***You probably developed this fear as a kid - it's not your fault.***
- ***It's in your DNA to have a natural fear of injections - thanks Evolution!***

As I said previously, knowledge is power. I've been doing this a long time and if you tell me that the above points don't make you feel a whole lot better then, **I wouldn't believe you!**

I want you to consider something else as well; it might not actually be the needle itself that is the origin of the problem. The needle may just REPRESENT the underlying issue. It doesn't really matter anyway because dealing with the object will dissolve the underlying issue anyway.

It could be one or a combination of some of the following:

- **Venephobia** – the fear of veins. This results in not even being able to look at your own veins or even allowing anyone to touch your wrists or neck where veins are closer to the surface of the skin.
- **Iatrophobia** – fear of doctors. This can also include nurses and is sometimes referred to as 'White Coat Syndrome'.
- **Dentophobia** – fear of Dentists including the smells, noises and tools associated therein.
- **Nosocomephobia** – fear of hospitals. Again, this includes all of the smells, images and accoutrements.
- **Hemophobia** – fear of blood. Not just that of the person with the phobia but ALL blood.
- **Algophobia** – fear of pain. Injections don't hurt but they represent the pain that goes with the relevant procedure, whether it's an operation or a dental procedure.

- **Thanatophobia** – the fear of death or dying. If you trace all phobias high enough they all lead to Rome (or death in this instance).

In my experience every needle phobic I have met has also suffered with at least one of the above. As previously mentioned, my first experience with Trypanophobia was my niece. She had an extreme needle phobia but she also couldn't even look at her own veins. Another issue she had was that she couldn't touch her own wrist and became apoplectic if someone else touched them. It had caused issues within the relationship with her partner. This was great from my perspective because it gave me a really clear tool to monitor our progress. We're close and she trusts me implicitly so I decided to try something that I wouldn't do with a regular client, I asked her to shake my hand but I reached further and brushed her wrist. Her response was extreme and very real. I pretended it was an accident. I don't think she believed me - we spend our lives joking around with each other so I got away with it. She asked if I could get rid of her wrist phobia after I've sorted out the needle thing. I agreed.

We were at my sister's house (her mum) and she happened to have a printer refill kit which contained a syringe and blunt needle. I told my Niece my plan of 'Systematic Desensitisation' (I'll explain later). I asked her where I could stand with the needle in my hand that would not cause her undue anxiety... So I started off the session standing at the end of the garden...

After about half an hour she stood there with a blank expression on her face holding the tip of the blunt needle against her arm. I exaggeratedly jumped up and down with my arms in the air which made her laugh. I told her she was the champion and grabbed her arm and held it in the air like a victorious boxer. I stood there with a smile on my face staring into her eyes. They went from amusement to confusion; she knew I was up to something. We both slowly gazed up at my hand clasping her wrist and she looked back at me and just shrugged with a smile on her face.

Remember: You will need to take full accountability for your own actions during this programme and that includes being creative when working with other people. It also requires you to be responsible for your own safety and you need to abide by the local rules regarding social distancing (if relevant). Remember: you are doing this to ensure your long-term health and safety so there's no point if you are risking you or your loved ones' short-term wellbeing!

Quick Quote...

"If you could read minds and listened to the absolute rubbish other people stress and worry about I reckon you'd feel so much better about yourself."

–Karl Rollison

CHAPTER SIX

BACK AND FORTH

From a simplistic perspective (without getting too deep or spiritual) there are just two states of existence, just two! Moving forward or moving backwards.

You might say,

"'AHH, got you there! You can stay where you are. You can stand still!"

And I would say,

"Staying where you are takes no effort. When you don't put anything in you can't expect anything out...STAYING WHERE YOU ARE IS MOVING BACKWARDS."

If we were to put live human cells in a Petri dish and put nutrients on one side of the dish and toxins on the other, what do you think would happen? I'll tell you, the cells would move towards the food and away from the danger.

So basically we are dealing with two states, moving **forwards** or moving **backwards**. Moving backwards is **protection,** and equates to our **'fight or flight'** instinct, whereas moving forwards is **growth** which engages our' **rest and digest'** system. The thing is, we can't do both at the same time.

Here's the other really important thing: Moving backwards or staying still is EASY! It's like hiding. It takes no energy. However, it's REALLY good at generating something. You want to know what? I'll tell you...

REGRET!!!

Don't take my word for it, do your own research. The best people to take advice from are the ones that have relevant experience, in this case, people who have conveyed their regrets when it's too late to do anything about it.

I'm talking about DEATHBED regrets...

Here is a list of the top ones from around the world:

1. ***Holding onto grudges.***
2. ***Ignoring own feelings.***
3. ***Not travelling enough.***
4. ***Spending too much time worrying.***
5. ***Not being honest with myself.***
6. ***Not taking enough chances.***
7. ***Not taking more care of my body.***

So, unless you are actually reading this on your deathbed, it's NOT too late to change. You should be really proud of yourself because you are already doing SOMETHING to change not just TALKING about it. The problem is...

You're not quite there yet.

The last stage of this book involves facing your nemesis.

It always amazes me when people are shocked that eradicating a phobia actually involves FACING the phobia. I mean what did they expect? There are no magic bullets, or magic wands. The real magic is in the actual doing. Because that' buzz' of adrenaline you're going to experience when you realise you have conquered your fears IS the magic.

Just bear this in mind:

You cannot grow in comfort. You just can't. It's not possible. The ONLY way you can move forward is by stepping out of your comfort zone...By stepping away from the cosy and familiar.

Scared now? Good!

"If you have fears and you let them hold you back, you are a worrier. If you let them push you forward, you are a warrior!"

–Karl Rollison

You should be doing this whole process in the safety, comfort and warmth of your own home. Following the processes in this book cannot harm you in anyway but I can guarantee NOT following them will. As I've already said, I will repeat myself and remind you of our agreement. Just stick with it. I want to quickly show you what's possible with a bit of belief and a sprinkling of visualisation.

(Safety first: don't attempt this exercise if you have a back problem).

THE POWER OF VISUALISATION AND BELIEF

Stand with you feet shoulder width apart and raise your right arm in front of you. Now point your index finger. Look along the length of your arm and along to the tip of your finger.

Now slowly turn to the right looking down the length of your finger. Keep turning until you physically can't turn any further. Make a mental note on the wall of the distance you achieved. Try this again; keep going until you can't go any further. Again make a mental note. Don't move your feet and try it once more, it'll probably be around the same point. This point represents your physical limit, your 'Nocebo'.

Now we are about to generate a 'Placebo' using visualisation and suggestion.

Stay relaxed and keep standing in the same position. Take a deep breath, hold it and let it out until your lungs are completely empty. Breathe normally and close your eyes. With your eyes closed keep your arms by your side. I want you to **imagine** that your spine is now made of rubber. Your whole body is hyper flexible. With your eyes closed imagine holding your arm and finger out in front of you as before. Visualise looking along the length of your arm as before. Now start to turn. Imagine that you are slowly moving round and see your finger stop at the point you got to last time. Now see your arm continue past that point and on. Keep going right round. You are made of rubber. Keep going right round until you almost reach the front again having almost done a 360 degree turn. Now open your eyes lift your arm and point your finger forward as before. Slowly turn around until you can't go any further.

I bet you are shocked at how much further you managed to go right? How amazing is that? Using visualisation you can achieve anything. When you accept this fact, you can change your beliefs! You'll need to remember this for the forthcoming fight...

CHAPTER SEVEN

CALIBRATION

"You can't manage what you can't measure"

- Peter Drucker

In other words, how do you know if you are moving forwards or backwards if you haven't got some form of reference point?

As a hypnotherapist and life coach, one of the key things in my toolbox is '***calibration***'. No two sessions I've ever had are the same, but calibration is the ONLY constant, it's the only thing I use in EVERY session regardless of what it is. Whether I'm helping people with anxiety, stress, trauma or confidence, I always calibrate. For you to safely and comfortably dissolve your phobia you're going to have to use it too. Don't worry it's simplicity itself.

You are the ONLY person on this planet that knows how you truly feel. You could be cross analysed by a team of the top experts in the world from a whole host of various fields using every technique, observation, drug and technology available but they still wouldn't know a fraction of how you really feel. **You are the ONLY true expert on you.**

When you are faced with your phobia you know exactly how you feel. So let's set up a scale of your phobia response, a '**Phobia-meter**'.

If you were relaxing on your sofa with a partner watching your favourite film waiting for the pizza to be delivered you'd probably be pretty low in anxiety. (Unless you had a pizza phobia – IMAGINE THAT!?). Let's put this as a zero on your phobia scale.

Now imagine the most anxious you've ever felt, where you were absolutely terrified. Your heart was racing, you were hyperventilating, you felt physically sick and your legs turned to jelly...This would be a 10 on the scale.

When I was working on my niece's phobia the only way we could get to a zero with a needle in my hand was if I was actually, physically away from the house.

I would have to leave the needle in the garden.

<u>SAFETY FIRST</u>

As I mentioned earlier, if you were sitting in front of me I'd be monitoring every aspect of you, including:

- Body posture.
- Breathing pattern.
- Fidgeting, rubbing and scratching.
- Lip and skin pallor.
- Hand movements and position.
- Jaw clenching.
- Amount of sclera visibility (whites of the eyes).
- Feet position.
- Voice tonality (pitch).
- Voice tempo (speed).
- Voice timbre (quality of the actual words).

Some of this stuff is obvious and we all naturally use it to monitor others. Some of it is more subtle and we need to actively *look* for it. For example, the nasal membrane is full of blood vessels close to the surface of the skin and, an itchy nose is a sign of elevated blood pressure, indicting anxiety.

As a side note: I've taught and studied Martial Arts most of my life and I've worked with the Police and security staff - if someone is visually agitated and staring at you, showing a lot of sclera (eye white) with red ears and they keep touching their nose – you're about to be attacked!

I mentioned previously that I got rid of my phobia by using a system called 'Flooding'. It was very uncomfortable and VERY stressful and I would NEVER recommend this to anyone. I was in full fight or flight mode and it took all of my self control to override the urge to run away. As, I mentioned, massive changes in blood pressure can cause Vasovagal Syncope (fainting).

HOWEVER...

What YOU'RE going to be using is a nice, safe and relaxing system that operates at your own pace called 'Systematic

Desensitisation'. In order to do this, you will have to take full responsibility, be 100% honest and constantly monitor how you feel on the scale we mentioned from 0 to 10.

So, what would give you a massive amount of anxiety? What would raise the number of your phobia gauge right up to a 10? Would it be holding a needle in your hand or is it so bad that just an image of a needle makes you sweat? Maybe you can't even say the word 'needle' without feeling uncomfortable – I've encountered that a few times. How about the cartoon-like rendering I drew for the cover of this book? How does that make you feel?

Whatever it is, you'll need to do some calibration. We use these numbers to directly correspond to the stage of Systematic Desensitisation. But before we do that we need to make sure that your ducks are in a row first*.

So, ideally this next section should be done with another person and you should ALWAYS be seated where possible.

Remember: You will need to take full accountability for your own actions during this programme and that includes being creative when working with other people. It also requires you to be responsible for your own safety and you need to abide by the local rules regarding social distancing (if relevant). Remember: you are doing this to ensure your long-term health and safety so there's no point if you are risking you or your loved ones' short-term wellbeing!

*no ducks will be harmed during this process.

Quick quote...

"Rather than looking to add things to your life that make you feel good, simply eliminate things that make you feel bad." *–K.Rollison*

CHAPTER EIGHT

GET YOUR DUCKS IN A ROW

If you're not familiar with this expression "Get your ducks in a row", don't worry, it just means:

"To make all the preparations needed to do something; get everything organised"

So what I'm talking about is to make sure that you are COMPLETELY sold on this programme, that you are totally engaged in the result. That there is no part of you that is in doubt. That you are not saying one thing and your body is telling me another.

If I was in front of you I'd be watching everything about you (not in a creepy way). I would get you comfortable. Sit opposite you and ask you a question then look over to my right (your left) and watch you with my peripheral vision. As a Language and Behaviour profiler I'd be watching to see if all your ducks are in a row, to see if your body language marries up to your words.

From a physiological perspective I'd be checking that you were fully ***'CONGRUENT'***.

An example of someone being INCONGRUENT is when you ask someone how they are and they say...

"Yeah, I'm really good, thanks for asking"

But as they say it they slightly shake their head from side to side.

They are TELLING you that they are fine but their body language is SHOWING you that they are not. This is your unconscious mind expressing itself and it never lies! This is how polygraph machines work.

I love people watching, especially in bars, pubs and restaurants. I watch out for the people on dates. I look out for the people who laugh out loud but they are not laughing with their eyes. The people whose spine is in an 'S' shape leaning back rather than a 'C' shape leaning forward towards the person opposite. The girl at the bar whose face might be pointing at the man she's talking to but her feet are pointing at the exit.

The thing is, if you came to me with a relationship issue, or you want help making a big decision or you wanted to get rid of something (or someone) out of your life, I would use this test to do an ECOLOGY check. To see that dissolving the said issue serves a purpose. That this really is the best thing for you and that it's SAFE to get rid of it.

I find these tests particularly useful when a client comes to see me because SOMEONE ELSE wants them to address an issue.

A few years ago I was at a party and I met a couple who I hadn't seen for a while. We were in the garden and the woman pointed at her husband and urged me to stop him smoking.

"Does HE want to give up?"

"Yeah, of course he does. He says so all the time".

So, she called him over.

I stood in front of him. Looked him square in the eyes and said **"Listen Geoff, I'm going to ask you something REALLY important right now and I want you and your unconscious mind to both answer me with 100% honesty…WOULD YOU LIKE TO BE A NON SMOKER".** I then looked away slightly.

He shot her a brief sideways look, there was a tiny delay before his voice went up a few octaves and he responded with a…

"Yeah" but it was more like a "Yeeaah?" It was more like a question than an answer.

Sally, a highly intelligent woman (although in a state of 'refreshment') turned to me and said,

"Told ya Karl"

I nearly spat out my Babycham. Was she joking? I have rarely ever seen a 'YES' that was so obviously a 'NO'.

A large percentage of being a good listener is just about paying attention to the details!

Another thing this highlights is that you can't impose your desires on others. No one has full control over anyone else. As the coolest actor of all time, Morgan Freeman observed in Bruce Almighty, (and another reason I need YOU to commit personally) – not even God can mess with free will!

You see a lot of our habits and behaviours serve a purpose on some level so you have to check that you really don't want or need it anymore!

EXCEPT WHEN IT COMES TO NEEDLE PHOBIAS THAT IS! IT IS SAFE TO SAY THAT YOUR LIFE WILL DEFINITELY IMPROVE WITHOUT IT!!!

So, I need to make sure you are fully congruent in this process...I know what you're thinking. You're thinking, *I am congruent and I do want to get rid of this phobia so I can skip this section.* Well, you've signed my agreement so, no you can't. You will have to follow this section to the LETTER as you agreed!

So your designated partner is going to be asking you the questions in this chapter and you are going to answer them **out loud with feeling, and emotion!**

Remember, everything in this book is relevant.

No one is going to see you do this and I'm not like one of those loud American TV Evangelists, am I?

"LET ME HEAR YOU SAY YEAH!!!"

Only joking.

STEP 1

So, with your partner, sit in a room where you won't be disturbed. Both sit comfortably. The person asking the question needs to just pay attention to you. People think there's magic to being able to gauge someone. There isn't, it's all about paying attention and using your instincts. This is the basis of human interaction and you've been doing it all your life, now you just have a specific reason to do it...

The person asking the questions really needs to take notice of your reactions. Really try to spot the difference between a' yes' and a 'no' response.

You should note how the questions make you feel.

Be honest with each other.

Ask the following questions:

First a ridiculous question with a definite NO response:

"Were you born on planet Mars?"

Then a question with a definite YES response:

"Do you live on Planet Earth?"

If you can't gauge the difference between both responses keep asking questions. Try to tune into the response. THIS IS REALLY IMPORTANT.

Now the big question:

"Do you really want to get rid of this needle phobia?"

"Do you really want to allow yourself to no longer fear needles?"

"Do you value your health more than you value your fear of a needle?"

"Do you love your family more than you fear a needle?"

"Is this needle phobia REALLY holding you back?"

"Are you READY to let this phobia go?"

The person asking the question should mark down any answers that aren't 100% and ask them again. This time, emphasise different parts of the question. Do this 3 times, i.e...

'Do **YOU** love your family more than you fear a needle?"

'Do you **LOVE** your family more than you fear a needle?"

'Do you love your family more than you **FEAR** a needle?"

STEP 2

Now you have answered the questions I want you to be animated about it. Remember, you've agreed to follow my rules.

Only we have experienced everything we have, and only we truly know how we feel. The key thing is tuning into the unconscious mind. Sometimes it's difficult to hear it, so we can ask it direct questions. As a hypnotherapist I use this system of speaking directly to the unconscious mind all the time. I ask it a question and ask for the response to be non-verbal, but a muscle movement instead. It's called 'Ideomotor Response' or IMR. 'Ideo' means idea and 'motor' means muscle movement so it literally means how a thought (usually prompted by a question) will evoke a certain, unconscious muscle response. We are basically bypassing the conscious mind.

What's really cool about IMR is that we can use it on ourselves at any time whilst we are awake. This really comes into its own when applied to decision making. Remember what we said in Chapter Six about human cells in a Petri dish? Cells will move towards nutrients and away from toxins. Well, guess what? WE are comprised of about 70 trillion of those cells and we have the same unconscious response to our environment, we naturally move away from danger and towards nourishment.

Imagine standing in front of a table, feeling hungry and there is a plate covered by a shiny metal Cloche (like you get in room service). We don't know what's under the cover but we are asked to remain as still as possible. The cover is removed revealing a sea of writhing maggots. We would move backwards, even if we tried not to. What about if the dish contained lovely, fresh, warm cakes? Chances are we would move forwards. These movements would be outside of our awareness.

This would be an example of our unconscious mind trying to either protect or nourish us.

IMR – THE LEARNING TEST

OK, so find somewhere quiet, where you feel safe and comfortable.

You'll need to be nice and relaxed.

The floor needs to be flat and even. First off you need to get a feel for the technique.

Take your shoes off and stand with your feet shoulder width apart and allow your arms to hang by your sides.

Now think of something you love. A person, a food, a place...try and get a clear image of it and say 'yes yes yes yes.'

Notice you are starting to lean forwards?

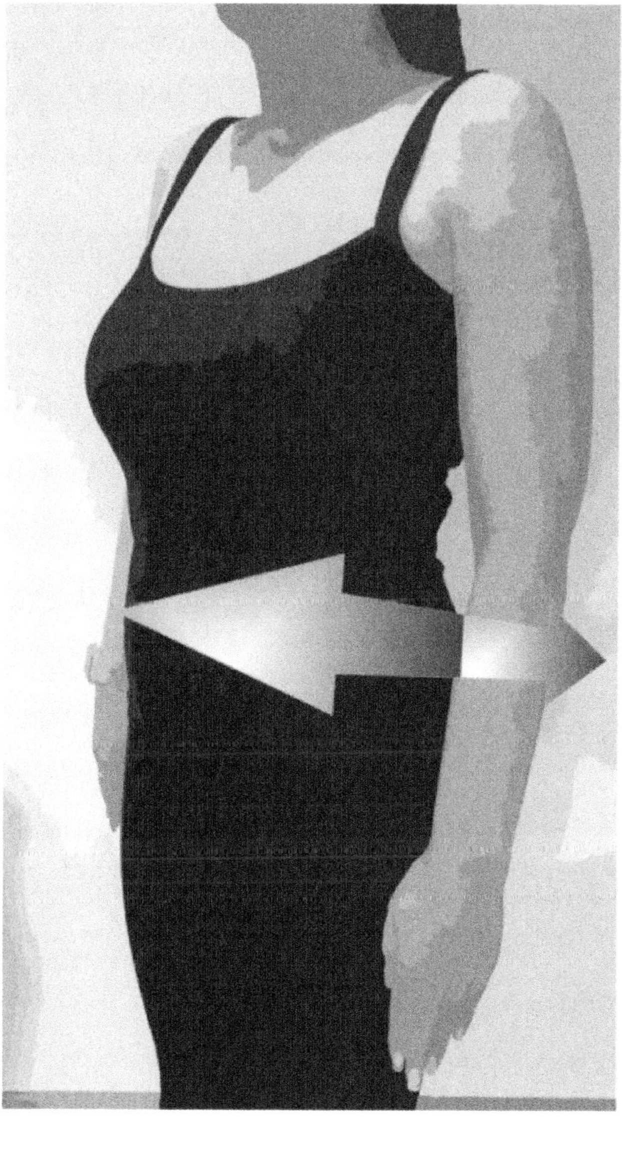

Now walk around the room and take some deep breathes (this acts as a reset).

Stand as you were before, but this time think of something you hate, something repulsive, a food, a place, Tony Blair, anything. This time say 'no no no no.'

Notice how you start to lean back?

Now you know how the technique feels. Walk around the room taking nice relaxing deep breaths. Think about something you're not sure about. A decision you need help with. Say out loud, for example, 'Is this person good for me?' It needs to be a clear question that requires a distinct yes or no answer. Sometimes the answers take a bit of bravery to acknowledge.

So, using the leaning method answer the questions again from stage 1 and, NO, you can't skip this bit!

You'll soon be able to FEEL just how much you and your unconscious mind are in agreement about the irrelevance of your needle phobia!

Don't underestimate the power of this technique. There are some highly influential people around the world making important decisions every day using this method.

CHAPTER NINE

HOW DARE YOU?!

OK so now...

- You understand WHY you have this phobia.
- You understand where it came from.
- You know where it's going (in the bin).
- You know that you definitely don't need it anymore.
- Your conscious mind doesn't want this phobia.
- Your UNCONSCIOUS mind doesn't want it.
- Your whole system is now fully aligned to eject it.
- The gun is fully loaded and ready to be fired.

So everything is in alignment that needs to be. You are aware of your issue...Time to get serious.

I've spent most of my adult life studying and teaching Martial Arts all over the world, including Japan on a number of occasions. I've also taught women's self defence and awareness. When I have a class of women in front of me, I want them to get proactive and strategic. Some self defence systems encourage anger in response to an attack but I don't think this is very effective. Anger is a really powerful emotion and can be associated with frustration and despair. This can also turn into tears, and tears aren't really useful in self defence. I've also experienced Women hitting the bag or focus mitts and losing punching power because they forgot why they were angry. You need to address a different and even more powerful weapon- ***INDIGNATION.***

'Indignation is anger or annoyance provoked by what is perceived as unfair treatment.'

I see indignation as anything that provokes a...

"HOW DARE YOU!?" response.

It could be something everyday like the following:

- You've been waiting in a queue for hours and someone blatantly pushes in front of you.
- It's been a hard day and you just want to get home but someone has parked in your allocated parking space.
- You receive an aggressive formal letter threatening legal action for a bill you have definitely paid.

- You've spent weeks on a project at work and your boss takes all the credit without acknowledging you.
- You go out of your way to help someone and you don't even get a 'Thank You'.

It could be a more extreme version:

- Someone bumps into your on the street and you later realise that you've been pickpocketed.
- Someone pulls a knife and takes your wallet and phone.
- You are the victim of a violent, unprovoked attack and you end up in hospital.
- A loved one has been attacked.
- A close family member has been run over on a pedestrian crossing by a drunk driver (this is one I can relate to).

This is a lot milder than the real-life, women's self defence provocation I've used to generate some serious indignation. I'll use highly graphic and gratuitous language and scenarios to generate some genuine, low-down, hi-torque indignation-driven, raw power...definitely best if I leave it to your imagination.

Anyway, I want to generate some raw power in you...

I want you to imagine that your phobia has manifested itself into human form. Think of someone you ***really dislike***. It could be:

- A colleague.
- Your boss.
- An ex-partner.
- A family member.
- A school bully.
- A former school teacher.
- That traffic warden.
- A neighbour.

If you can't think of anyone in your real life think of someone in the media.

- An actor.
- A sports personality.

- A reality Star.
- An 'Influencer'.
- A YouTuber.
- A politician.
- A musician.

Now you have a name for your phobia. I want you to imagine that person standing there shouting at you. It could be in any situation you can imagine. It could be in the workplace, a field, a car park, in a boxing ring. Now think how they appear. I want you to imagine them trying to belittle you at every level - they are prancing in front of you dressed in a giant hypodermic needle fancy dress.

I used this system in Harley Street with a nice, polite, mature woman who had an extreme wasp phobia. It was so bad that she had rarely been to a park, pub garden or BBQ. It was a lovely day so it took 10 minutes for her to sit down in my office because my window was open displaying a beautiful flower box which was a source of interest for the local insects.

Here's a quick example of my favourite style of coaching – Provocative Therapy, trying to illicit a response.

"Your window is open?" She nervously observed.

"I know, isn't it a gorgeous day?"

"What... what if a wasp comes in?"

"Oh, don't worry, I like wasps"

"No but seriously, would you not be shocked if one flew in?"

"I'd be more shocked if one DROVE in."

Anyway, we did some work (pretty much what you've done so far) and I decided to finish the session in Regents Park which is 5 minutes walk from the office. She imagined that her phobia was represented by her ex-husband, Ian.

So, I loaded her up with indignation and scoped the area for her phobia. She was getting animated and as the adrenaline built up she handed me her handbag in case she spilt its contents. We found some wasps innocently going about their business by one of the bins. She completely threw me off guard. She shoved me out of the way, put her fists on her hips ala Superman, bent down face to wasp and screamed at the top of her voice...

"F***k off Ian! Leave me alone!" This attracted a fair bit of attention.

Some big bloke walking his equally big dog started marching over and I found myself reassuring him that I wasn't Ian by bizarrely pointing at the ladies handbag I was holding.

So I want you to imagine your nemesis in whatever way possible to generate as much power as you can. I want you to imagine them smirking at you. Think about their mannerisms. Really try to recall EXACTLY how they sound. Imagine them looking you up and down and arrogantly sneering:

- **I'm the reason people think you're a joke.**
- **You're so scared of me that you won't get that health issue looked at.**
- **I'm the reason you've got that pain.**
- **I'm here to stop you having that blood test.**
- **You're pathetic!**
- **I control everything you do.**
- **I can stop you getting that inoculation!**
- **Want to do your bit and give blood? Tough!**
- **Want to travel and see the world? You'll need lots of vaccinations! Forget it!**

So, if someone was following you around telling you what you could and couldn't do, where you could and couldn't go and who you could and couldn't associate with, you'd soon tell them where to go wouldn't you!?

Right then, we've done most of the ground work it's nearly time for the final stage. If you think I've just been waffling on and you've just been reading some weird stuff out of a book that hasn't been written using a hypnotic framework laced with embedded commands, subliminal suggestions and metaphors then I've achieved my aim...

CHAPTER TEN

GET ORGANISED

A few years back this lovely 72 year old chap nervously walked into my office with his equally lovely wife. We'd already had a bad-quality FaceTime consultation and they had signed my terms and conditions. There was no payment due because, well, the simple answer is that...

I've never actually charged for a needle phobia!

Thinking that someone would quietly suffer in pain because they couldn't afford my services would keep me awake at night.

"Karl, you said on the call that I'd need to do some strange things. I am absolutely ready to do anything and everything but I have to be careful dancing because I have a bad knee."

"Dancing?! I will definitely ask you to do some weird stuff but no dancing mate. What gave you that idea?"

"Didn't you mention something about Tap dancing?" he anxiously looked at his wife.

She nodded and rubbed her mouth with confused concern but I think she was actually trying not to laugh.

"I said TAPPING not TAP DANCING!"

I was so pleased I could help these wonderful people but what really impressed me was the fact that this amazing man was willing to do ANYTHING to address his phobia. For all he knew I was going to ask him to tap dance up Regent Street, but he STILL made an appearance.

So there's no dancing involved but there is a lot of tapping. What IS tapping? First I need to tell you something **REALLY important...**

Throughout history, Western science and medicine have been firmly based on **'Newtonian'** physics, i.e., dealing with what you can see and feel in front of you. However, over the last hundred years there has been a distinct shift towards **'Quantum'** physics. This teaches us that, what we experience in the physical realm is merely the surface. Everything is, in fact, comprised of pure energy: the universe, the planets, the oceans, your cat and, of course, you...***Everything*** about you, including your thoughts and emotions. Traditional Eastern medicine has been working with this system for over 5000 years. The energy in your body is known as 'Chi' (Chinese) or 'Ki' (Japanese) but different cultures have different variants. Just like wire carries electricity, your body transmits this energy via channels called **'Meridians'**. This system can be controlled by manipulating key areas or **'pressure points'**. Now, one way of doing this is via '**Acupuncture'** which was developed in China 200 years BC and, don't forget, Acupuncture was only accepted in the West around 50 odd years ago - up until then it would have been dismissed as nonsense. **'Acupressure'** is a form of non-intrusive meridian manipulation that relies on finger pressure rather than needles.

Another version of Acupressure is **'Tapping'**. This is a highly effective system for dealing with all forms of negativity. It was developed in the mid 1980s by the late American psychologist Dr Roger Callahan.

You'll also be using another form of meridian therapy called **'Jin Shin Jyutsu'** which dates back over a thousand years. As well as this, there'll be some breathing techniques. Any of the above techniques can be used to successfully eradicate a phobia but when combined into a therapy cocktail they are particularly powerful.

Before we get started I need to put the last piece of the puzzle into place to make sure you are totally ready. This is the last of the prep work...

THE NIGHT BEFORE NMP (No More Phobia)

So you've set aside a day for NMP. You're feeling ready. There is something important you need to ensure on the morning of the phobia day - you need to ensure that you are not 'Psychosocially Reversed'.

Psychosocially Reversal was also a concept developed by Roger Callaghan and it basically means that the sufferer is in a state of subconscious self-sabotage. Most people experience varying degrees of PR throughout their life. Some people make it a perpetual habit. You know these people, just when they start to get sorted they seem to mess it all up. They usually go from job to job and relationship to relationship. These people feel uncomfortable with positive things in their lives.

You know when you're in a state of PR because you can FEEL it. Have you ever woken up on a fantastic holiday in a beautiful location with amazing weather and for some reason felt miserable? Well, you were probably reversed.

The things that can contribute to PR are:

- Drugs.
- Alcohol.
- Dehydration.
- Lack of sleep.
- Stress.

- Poor diet.
- Smoking.
- Caffeine.
- Excessive sugar consumption.

The night before NMP I need you to get a really good night's sleep. I want you to drink plenty of water and avoid alcohol in the night and avoid caffeine in the morning.

We then need to take things one stage further by doing the PR triangle. This involves tapping of the blade of the hand or the 'Karate Chop'. I need to mention thc power of this area...

As part of my journey over the years I've been involved in all the 'Empowering' exercise including:

- Fire walking.
- Punching out candle flames.
- Barefoot glass walking.
- Underwater meditation.
- Snapping arrows with the Neck.
- Board breaking.

I've even put my hand in liquid Nitrogen. All of these exercises are fantastic and really empowering but there's no magic involved. It's pure Science. The only time I've felt compelled to object was during a board breaking class – had everyone followed the trainers' instructions, there would have been a lot of people with long-term hand damage...

Like most people, perhaps you envisage a Karate chop delivered with a flat hand? Try to break a board with that and you'll (at the very least) bruise bones and damage the Ulna nerve. But with a tiny adjustment, you can do more damage, without injury, than a heavyweight boxer could with a punch! (Not telling you. This book is about healing not hurting).

So, this area (if used correctly) can deliver the most powerful strike a human can deliver with a naked hand with no injury. It can be used to easily knock someone out no matter how big they are. The conventional way of knocking someone out by hitting the jaw (hardest bone in the body) with the fist (a very delicate structure) usually ends in injury for both parties. The fist is only effective when the bones are bound (that's why boxers wear tight hand wraps). That's why one of the best boxers of all time, Mike Tyson, broke his hand in a street fight.

Another time I witnessed the power of the Karate chop area is my Nan (God bless her). I looked after her for a while when she was suffering with Dementia. She had endured pain all her life but she didn't like how painkillers made her feel so she would sit all day long tapping this area. All day long. I asked her why she did it.

"It's the only thing that takes the pain away".

"Who showed you how to do it Nan?"

"No one..."

So, the next time you have any form of pain, give it a go. It's free, non addictive and my Nan swore by it.

The PR Triangle

First off, make a note of how you feel.

Tap the Karate chop of one hand firmly with the fingers of the other hand.

Now keep tapping and say out loud:

I WANT to be needle phobia free!

I CAN be needle phobia free!

I WILL be needle phobia free!

I AM needle phobia free!

Then tap under the nose for 30 or so taps

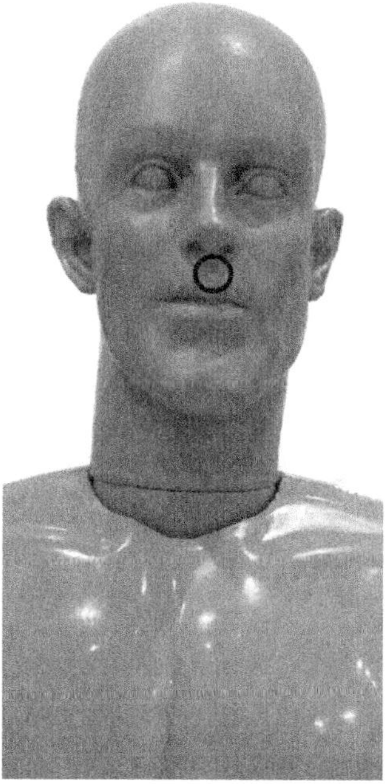 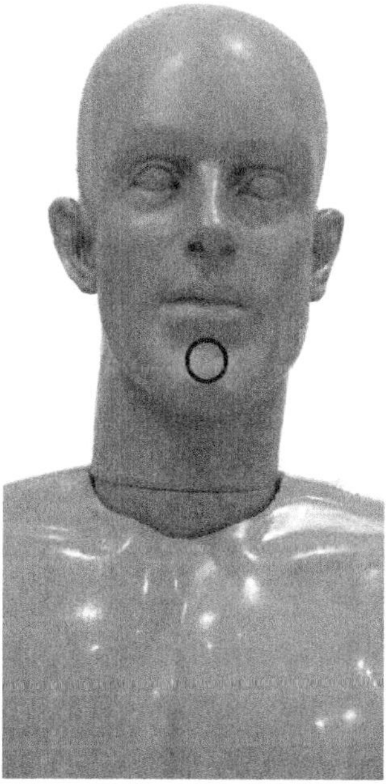

Now tap on the chin for 30 plus times

Then tap the Karate chop of the other hand and say out loud:

I WANT to feel even better!

I CAN feel even better!

I WILL feel even better!

I AM even better!

I'M OK!

Keep repeating the triangle. You will suddenly feel a positive shift.

Why not try the whole thing again? You can't OD on this stuff.

When I do this with people they usually take a sudden deep breath in through their nose. I won't go into why this happens but just accept that it feels great!

This system is really good for aligning your intentions and flipping into a positive mindset.

CHAPTER ELEVEN

READY...

So I haven't just got Bookish knowledge studied in a comfortable, warm classroom like some therapists out there. I've circumnavigated this planet twice and explored 50 countries looking for people to learn from. I've studied with priests, doctors, monks, Yogis, martial artists, boxers, spiritualists, stage hypnotists, hypnotherapists and a variety of different forms of therapies, both modern and ancient. I only show, use and write about empirical stuff – things I have witnessed, analysed, used and tested. I'm a natural sceptic and my first instinct when I see something new is, 'What a load of c**p!'

I have trained with my current martial arts instructor, Norman Smithers, for over 30 years and he is THE toughest human being I've ever known. Not only is he ex-Special Forces and a former French Foreign Legion Sergeant but he is also ranked Dai Shihan (one of the highest grades in Ninjutsu outside of Japan).

He calls me Son and I call him Dad and just like a real family relationship, we argue a lot. My first experience of meridian manipulation was many years ago with Norman. He was discussing Kyusho points (this is what Japanese call pressure points). All martial arts and Eastern medicines use these same points and, as I previously mentioned, they just call them different names. So I jumped in the middle of the Dojo in front of the class to be demonstrated on. I've always considered myself pretty tough and no matter how much pain I'm in or how much blood is involved I try to pretend I'm absolutely fine.

Norman struck me in the side of the neck (the carotid) with a Karate chop type strike called a 'Shuto'. Imagine loosely rattling some dice in your hand then lazily throwing them, that's the same motion.

So I felt the pressure in my head increase slightly and I definitely heard some ringing in my ears but it was nothing I couldn't handle.

"OK, so everyone made a note of how hard I hit Karl, yes?"

nods from the class.

'Now, I'm going to hit him in the same spot only not as hard. But first I'll do this."

Norm pointed at his head and, as this was a demo, I threw a slow, clumsy jab whilst intentionally dropping my guard to accommodate the intended strike.

Norman intercepted my arm and ran his knuckles hard along a certain point on my arm (nope, not telling you), then struck me in the neck again in the same place with the same hand as before. I clearly remember seeing the strike come in with my peripheral vision (focal vision is great for reading and sowing but not fighting...bit like quality listening).

So, I tried not to smirk as it continued its arch. Then...BANG! It all went quiet...and...dark. I found myself looking up at the ceiling and that was that...

I tried to stand up and one of my 'mates' said something about 'Bambi on ice'.

Anyway, that was the moment I realised the absolute POWER of Kyusho points and meridian manipulation.

Here's a quick demo for you to try (it's not compulsory) and don't worry, it doesn't hurt.

Remember: you are responsible for your own safety and you need to abide by the local rules regarding social distancing.

Meridian demo

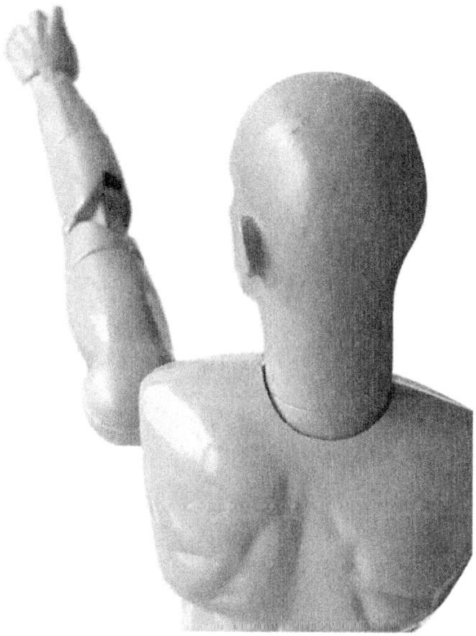

Get your partner to stand with their feet shoulder width apart.

Ask them to hold one arm out and gently clench their fist.

They should just hold their hand out and not tense up, just naturally support the weight of their own arm.

Gently push down on the back of their hand with your non-dominant hand and notice how much power is required to press the arm down.

Stand in front of them. Imagine that there is a strut protruding from their hip and attached to their arm, supporting its weight.

I want you to imagine that you are going to quickly swipe the support strut out of the way with your dominant hand and let their arm collapse.

Now quickly swing your hand under their outstretched arm and bat the imaginary support away with the palm of your hand but grab it on the way through. Try not to hit them in any way. With the strut held in your fist press down again with your 'empty' hand as before. Notice how much easier it is? There should be a HUGE difference.

You have just affected the meridian network of their body without touching them!

CHAPTER TWELVE

AIM...

So you now know how to do the PR triangle. Why not have another go now? It makes you feel great and it's free.

I want you to think about your **Phobia-Meter** again (page 64). Just refresh your mind and think about your level right now.

As mentioned, there are seven main techniques you will be utilising:

1. **The PR triangle. Page 104.**
2. **Systematic Desensitisation.**
3. **Calibration (Phobia-Meter). Page 64.**
4. **Tapping. Page 119.**
5. **Breathing. Page 117.**
6. **Thumb holding. This is coming up shortly.**
7. **Visualisation. That's a bit later on.**

This might sound complex but trust me, it really isn't!

1. The PR triangle takes seconds.

2. Systematic Desensitisation is exposing yourself to your fear at a rate that's comfortable to you. Using...
3. Calibration which is a number that represents how anxious you feel.
4. Tapping is isolating and manipulating key areas of the body at the appropriate time.
5. The breathing will be used as a RESET.
6. Thumb holding is a really simple very powerful technique to dissolve fear and...
7. You use visualisation on a DAILY basis anyway.

These are going to be used in a certain order. First off, I'm going to show you a lovely little technique that you can use at anytime whenever you feel worried or anxious, not just in the context of this book but ANYWHERE at ANYTIME, you can thank me later. This is a martial arts technique that derives from the art of Jin Shin Jyutsu - where different fingers relate to different parts of your bodies meridian network, and thus different emotions. This is a form of meridian therapy. Trust me, this stuff works! In Ninjutsu we work on meridian points

(Kyusho points) to cause damage when they are struck, but they can also heal when massaged.

The Thumb Anxiety Reducer

Spread the fingers of your dominant hand out.

Clamp the thumb with the other hand in a pincer motion and gently pull it down towards its palm. Don't grab it with your fist; forming a fist generates anger (think of road rage and trolley rage).

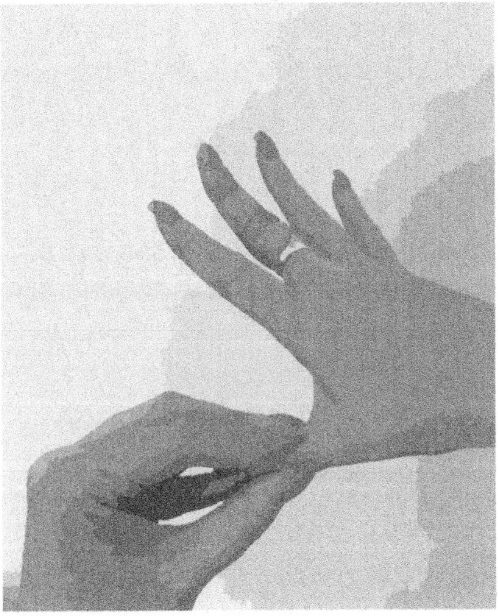

Hold this for about 90 seconds.

You should suddenly notice a change in your anxiety.

Do it for as long and as often as necessary. You can't overdose on this stuff.

I cured a chronic elevator phobia with this one technique.

Now, on to the breathing part of the programme, again this can be used anywhere at any time.

The 5/12 Breathing Technique

You can do this technique pretty much anywhere and, like any other technique, the more you do it the better you'll get.

Make a quick note of how stressed you feel right now from 0 to 10. (0 is not at all and 10 is extreme).

Sit in a quiet place where you can fully relax. Sit with your back straight.

Close your eyes and place your hands on either side of your stomach just under your ribs.

Keeping your eyes closed gently look up as though looking at the inside of your eyebrows.

Breathe in through your nose and at the same time imagine that you are breathing in through the back of your hands. This invites the abdomen and diaphragm to the party.

Breathe in deep and fill the lungs from top to bottom. Breathe in for the count of 5.

Pay attention to the pause between breaths.

Purse your lips and imagine you are trying to blow out a candle over the other side of the room. Breathe out of your mouth for the count of 12 or until your lungs are completely empty. If you do this right you will be aware of your stomach sucking in.

Repeat this as many times as you can but stop if you get dizzy.

Now, I want you to gauge your stress levels again from 0 to 10. If you have done this properly this level will be considerably lower! When you breathe out longer than you breathe in you are activating your parasympathetic nervous system. You are tipping your autonomic nervous system away from 'fight or flight' towards 'rest & digest.'

By the way, breathing with the stomach and really using the diaphragm might feel a bit odd at first, but guess what? That's how we ALL breathed when we were babies; we just forgot how to do it as we grew older. It amazes me to what extent everything involves breathing. It's the key to life and, as you'll see, it can be a really powerful tool. Yet most people go through their lives only thinking about breathing when they experience difficulties doing it. *I have an advantage over most people when it comes to appreciating breathing because when I was a little boy I nearly died from an extreme Asthma attack.*

Tapping

So now we'll cover the tapping aspect of the programme. I reckon you're ready so let's just get on with it.

The pressure required for effective tapping should be hard enough to feel it but not too hard that it leaves a bruise. Now you should tap each respective point approximately 20 times.

1. The first stage is to tap under the eye

The position is directly under the middle of the eye on the ridge of the orbital bone.

2. Now tap the collar bone. Where it meets the chest just below the bone knuckle.

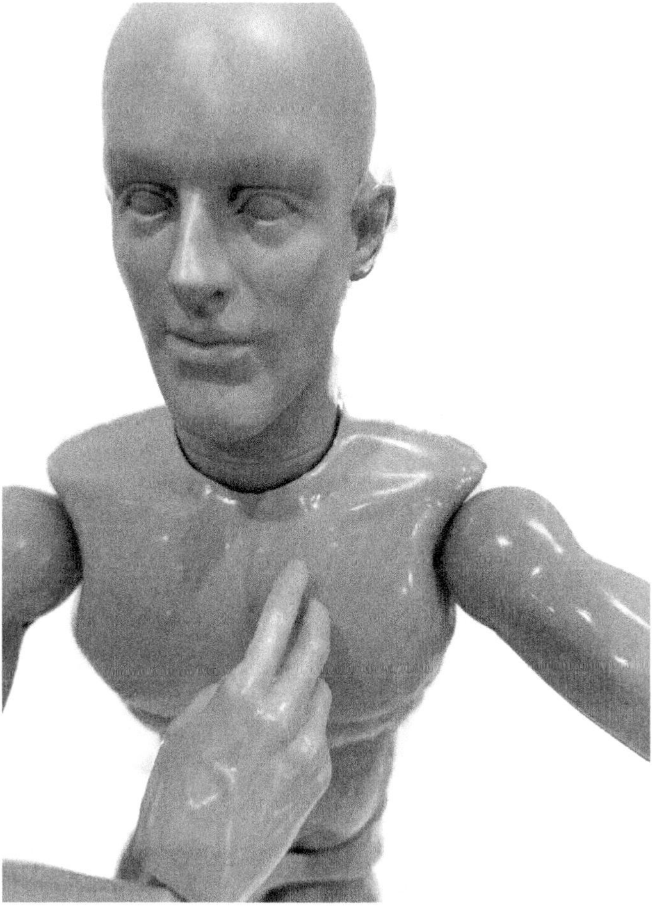

3. Now under the arm. Lift up your arm and place your fist in your armpit. Where your little finger touches your ribs on the seam of your clothes is the tapping point.

4. The next tap is the back of the hand between the bones of the little finger and the ring finger.

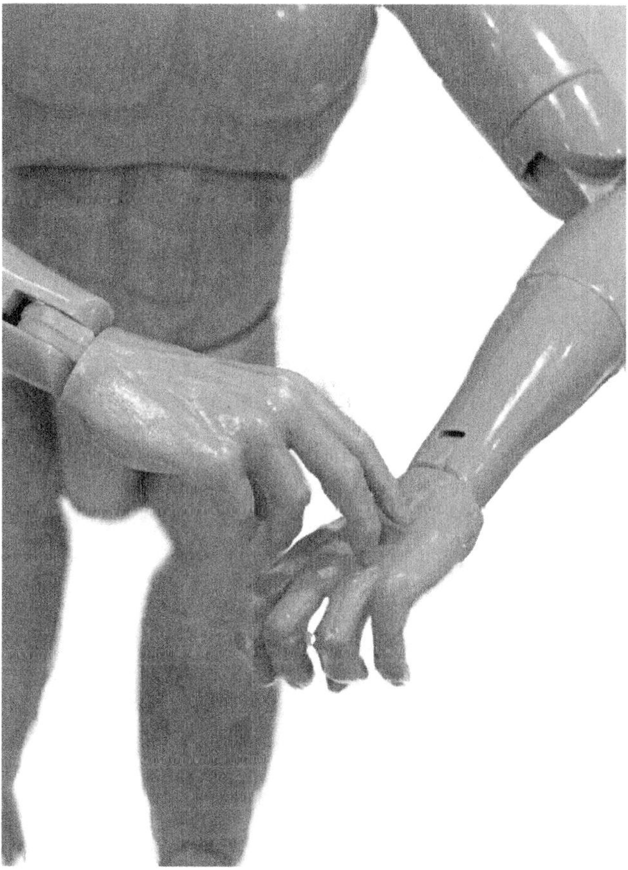

5. Whilst tapping this point look down to the left pause.

6. Then down to the right. Pause.

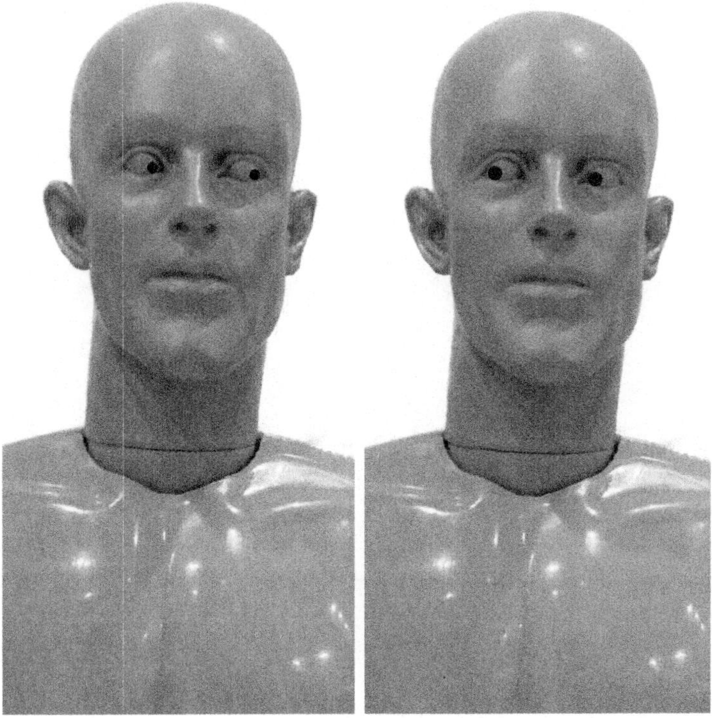

7. Then roll them wide around the left. Pause.

Then around to the right.

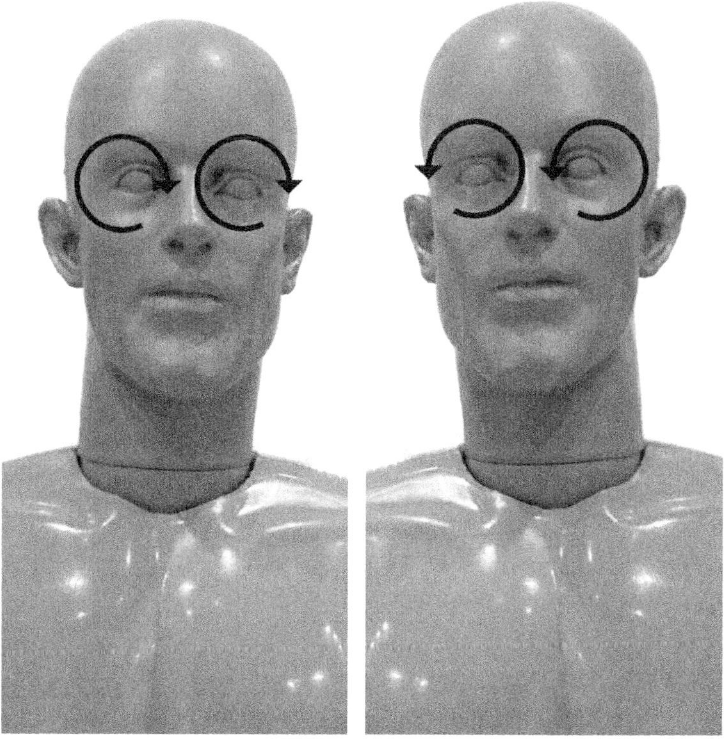

Remember you are still tapping the back of your hand.

Now count slowly to 10. Then slowly from 10 to 0.

Then hum 'Happy Birthday'. STOP TAPPING.

Told you it was weird, didn't I?

Now familiarise yourself with everything. It's time to kick the phobia's bottom.

Quick quote...

> *"We are like magnets. When we stress, we repel and when we relax, we attract."*
>
> *–Karl Rollison*

CHAPTER THIRTEEN

FIRE!!!

So, it's time!

Hopefully you have:

- **Rested well.**
- **Drunk plenty of water.**
- **Avoided alcohol.**
- **Avoided caffeine.**
- **Familiarised yourself with all the relevant techniques.**
- **Reserved the whole day for this exercise.**
- **Fully briefed your partner on their role.**
- **Dressed yourself in loose, comfortable clothes.**
- **A BLUNT needle and syringe.**

So let's start off with the PR triangle. You should know it by now but if not go to page **104** and spent as much time as you need until you feel ready.

You then need to get comfortable in the area where this activity is taking place. REMEMBER: to get the FULL benefit from this system you need to be inside with a partner.

ROUND 1

Your partner (**Person A**) needs to be in possession of the blunt syringe and needle. They will be inseparable for the duration of this procedure.

They need to position themselves where you are completely safe and secure and your Phobia-Meter (PM) is low.

You will need to be in communication with **Person A.** When I've done this I've sometimes had to shout my position but if there is a big distance between you both then you could use your phones. So **Person A** walks towards you and they need to say something sinister like '**Your injection is on its way'.**

YOU NEED TO BE CONSTANTLY MONITORING YOUR PM.

Let them approach you until your PM gets to about a 7 or until you are really uncomfortable but **DON'T ALLOW A PANIC ATTACK.**

REMEMBER: you are in charge and in full control of this process!

At the point you feel really uncomfortable, do the tapping procedure starting on page 119...

Person A then retreats but they need to set a marker on the floor of how far they got.

You can relax. Have a mouthful of water.

Do the breathing exercise on page 117 whilst holding your thumb (page 116).

ROUND 2

Start again. Ask **person A** to approach you until you feel an extreme response. Whether they are outside or inside the room allow them to approach until you can't handle it any more then. They should be closer than before.

Start tapping – page 119.

Tell them to retreat.

Sip some water.

Do the breathing exercise and the thumb pull (117, 116).

Do the PR triangle again (page 104).

Keep repeating the above until **Person A** is actually in the room with you. When they are in front of you I want you to look at the needle in their hand, if that's too much ask them to leave and start this round again.

Each time you take your PM to the maximum, the maximum will actually be lower than before.

YOU ARE IN CONTROL OF THIS WHOLE PROCESS USING YOUR PM AND THE AIM IS TO RID THE PHOBIA NOT JUST CAUSE STRESS!

ROUND 3

When **person A** is visible you should start to feel less anxiety around the sight of the needle. They should hold it aggressively, like they are approaching you to inject you.

I also want you to hear the voice of the needle threatening you.

Tap again (page 119) to lower your PM number.

Breathe (117). Thumb (116).

ROUND 4

Every time you feel uncomfortable you start tapping. You must allow the anxiety to get high but manageable. You will notice that each round your phobia levels drop. **THIS IS YOUR PHOBIA DYING!**

You should be at the stage where the person with the needle can slowly approach you. Remember you and your PM are in control.

Here's another thing I need you to do.

AS THE NEEDLE GETS CLOSER TO YOU, I WANT THE VOICE OF THE NEEDLE TO GET QUIETER AND HIGHER PITCHED. IT STARTS OFF LOUD BUT STARTS TO *BECOME A tiny Mickey Mouse voice.*

Repeating the above steps and applying the various relaxation methods where required should allow **Person A** to be standing over you with the needle in hand.

ROUND 5

I now want you to take the needle in your hand.

(If you need some assistance repeat round 4).

At this point you'll probably feel a sense of confusion. This is a good sign.

Take the needle in your hand and examine it. Do a combination of anything I've shown you to make yourself feel comfortable if needed (it won't be).

ROUND 6

When you feel ready, ask **person A** to hold the needle against your arm. This should now not be a problem.

I want you to start squeezing and releasing your fist. Get ready for the injection. I want you to smile and shrug.

With the blunt needle against your arm I want you to imagine that the roles have reversed: the syringe is now scared of YOU! You notice that it's trembling in fear of YOU. You also realise that it is now silent - IT HAS NOTHING TO SAY ANYMORE!

Lean forward and give it a piece of your mind. Whatever and however it comes out. Let some of the emotions out. Say something with gritted teeth like

“Not so cocky now are you?”

“Who’s in control now?”

“You’re pathetic!”

If there are tears then let them flow. You are releasing some powerful emotions. AND SO...

Believe it or not when you are at the stage of holding a needle (even though it’s blunt) against your vein with no reaction at all, **YOU’RE DONE!**

THAT’S IT!

Don’t forget, I’ve done this hundreds of times. If you have no reaction at that stage, then you’ve done it. You should be so proud of yourself!

You are now an expert on curing your own phobia.

Just one last thing now...

CHAPTER FOURTEEN

INTO THE FUTURE...

So, we now need to add the last component which is ***VISUALISATION.***

Do the breathing technique again whilst sitting down and close your eyes.

I want you to imagine you are going for your injection but the really IMPORTANT thing here is to not see yourself in the picture but to see the whole scene **THROUGH YOUR OWN EYES.**

I want you to think of this as a future memory that you are recalling, a memory that hasn't happened yet.

Visualise approaching the building and add as much sensory detail as possible:

- *Hear the sounds of the day, traffic, bird song, and people.*
- *Smell the air. Imagine breathing in deeply.*
- *Feel the temperature of the environment.*

- *See the colours around you.*

I also want you to imagine what clothes you are wearing, who you are with and what you are talking about.

Now I want you to sit in the seat and imagine that the medical practitioner is about to inject you.

I need you to visualise the feeling of INDIFFERENCE to the situation. Imagine that you are feeling the same mild inconvenience as you would with any other of life's annoyances, like standing in a long queue or waiting in for a delivery.

Whilst you sit there, look over to anyone else in the room and, with a look of indifference, do an exaggerated shrug and say:

"WHO CARES?!"

So arrange that blood test, get that tooth looked at, book in for that operation or go for the COVID vaccination.

You're FREE!

On the day:

Take your partner and your techniques.

Take this book...if you feel the need to.

Listen to some classical music...if you feel the need to.

Chewing gum relaxes our nervous system so, chew gum...if you feel the need to.

The chances are you won't need any gimmicks. You'll just need YOU because YOU did this, no one else!

YOU SHOULD BE SO PROUD OF YOURSELF. GO AND SHOW THE WORLD HOW POWERFUL YOU ARE!!!

If you want an extra boost you could always do some or all of the exercises again. As I said, they are non-addictive, safe with zero side effects and what's more, they're free! (like you).

Closing question, the same one I asked at the beginning of this book. From a scale of 0 to 10 (0 being not at all and 10 being extreme) how bad is your phobia now?

Write the number here

Last quote...

> *"It amazes me that people go around believing in UFOs, Satan, God, Santa, ghosts etc, but in reality, the main thing people need to believe in is* ***themselves!****"*
>
> *–Karl Rollison*

NOTES

NOTES

OTHER TITLES BY THE AUTHOR

Stress Ninja

Sleep Ninja

Desk Stress (eBook)

All available on Amazon

STRESS NINJA ®

Printed in Great Britain
by Amazon

59219835R00081